How to use this book

1)The book is divided into 23 didactic units.
2) All instructions are written in English and Italian
3)Each unit is focused on a specific letter of the italian alphabet.
4)The Last unit is a summary of all units studied

Example of Unit

The letter a (La lettera a)

TITLE

ARANCIA

Practice and Fun (Esercizio e divertimento)

Colour the five pictures that begin with a.(Colora i 5oggetti che iniziano con a)

PRACTICE & FUN

Draw the sentence(Disegna la frase): Un'ape su un'arancia

DRAWING YOUR ITALIAN

Matteo Albarella is an italian writer and teacher. After his degree in Philosophy he continued his studies, getting a post graduated certification on Didactics of Italian as a Foreign Language. After that he has lived and studied in Uk and Spain as well.
On his long experience as an Italian teacher for foreigners, he has developed a particular attention to the teaching of a foreign language for kids.
At the moment he is a language consultant for Novartis pharma Spa and CEO of the online school: www.learnwithtaste.com

A
aereo

B
bandiera

C
casa

D
dado

E
elefante

F
farfalla

G
gatto

H
hotel

isola
I

L
libro

M
marinaio

nido
N

O
orologio

P
palla

quadro
Q

rospo
R

sole
S

T
tamburo

uva
U

V
vaso

zebra
Z

Exercise

Join up the pairs of letters. Colour each pair. (Collega le lettere uguali e colorale)

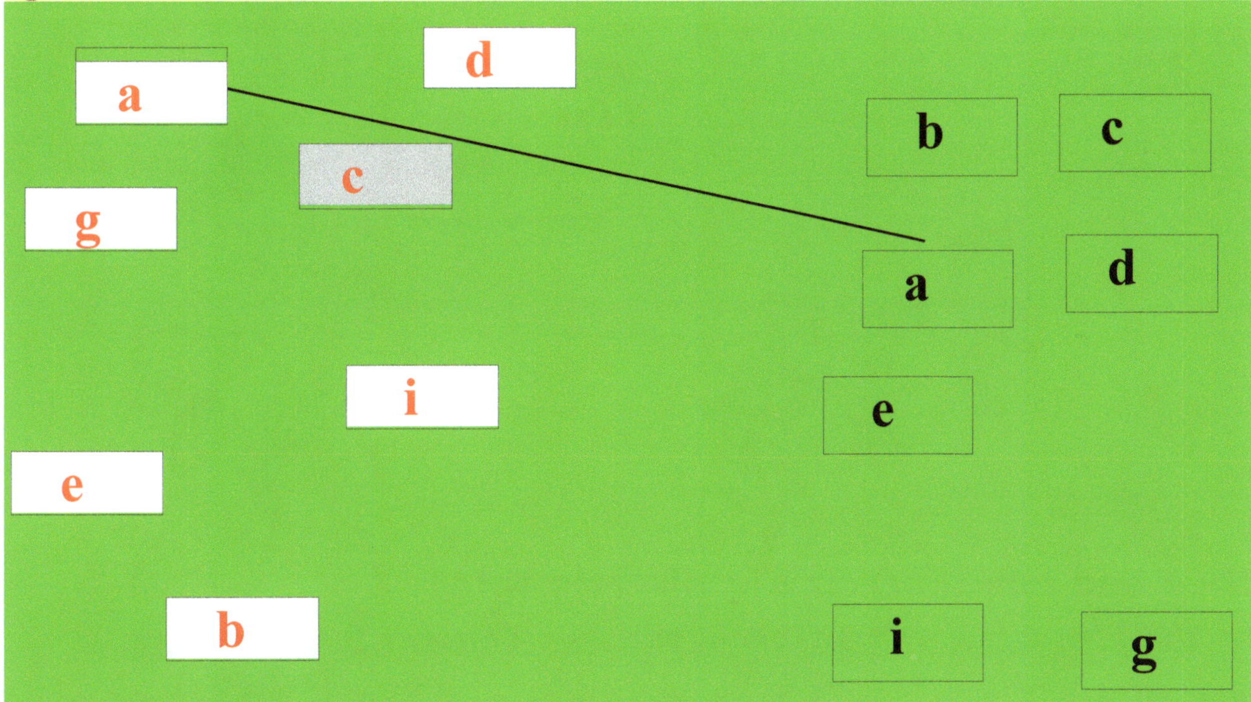

Practice and Fun (Esercizio e divertimento)

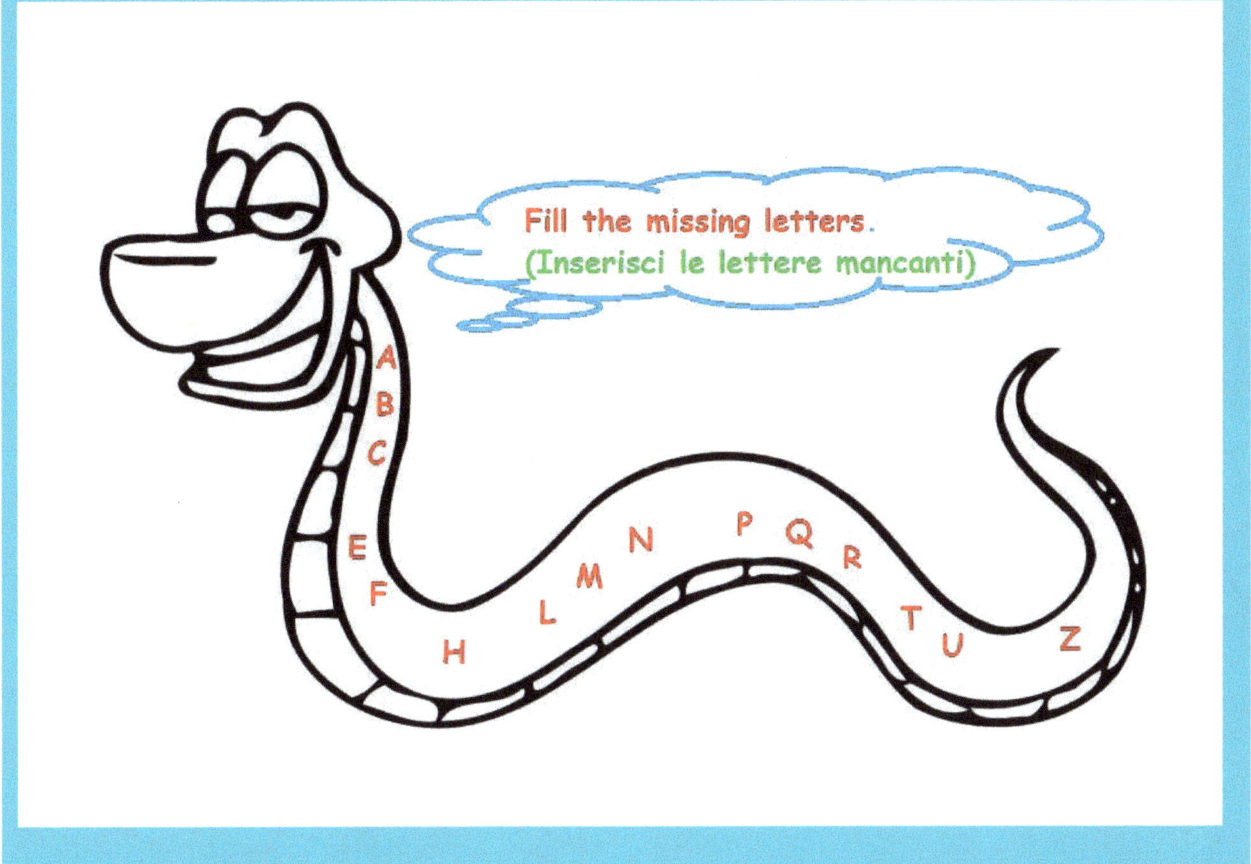

The letter a (La lettera a)

ARANCIA

Practice and Fun (Esercizio e divertimento)

Colour the five pictures that begin with a. (Colora i 5 oggetti che iniziano con a)

Draw the sentence (Disegna la frase): Un'ape su un'arancia

The letter b (La lettera b)
BOTTIGLIA

Practice and Fun (Esercizio e divertimento)

Colour the five pictures that begin with b. (Colora i 5 oggetti che iniziano con b)

B

Draw the sentence (Disegna la frase): Una borsa blu

The letter c (La lettera c)

CANE

Practice and Fun (Esercizio e divertimento)

Colour the five pictures that begin with c. (Colora i 5 oggetti che iniziano con c)

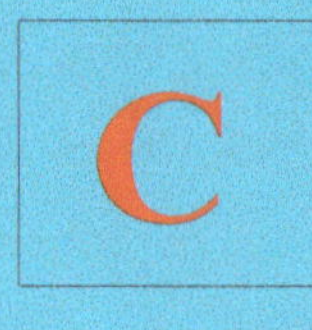

Draw the sentence (Disegna la frase):Un cane con un cappello

The letter d (La lettera d)

DELFINO

Practice and Fun (Esercizio e divertimento)

Colour the five pictures that begin with d. (Colora i 5 oggetti che iniziano con d)

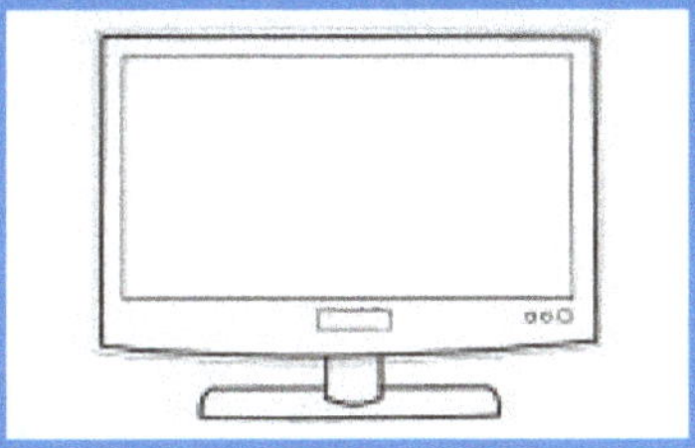

D

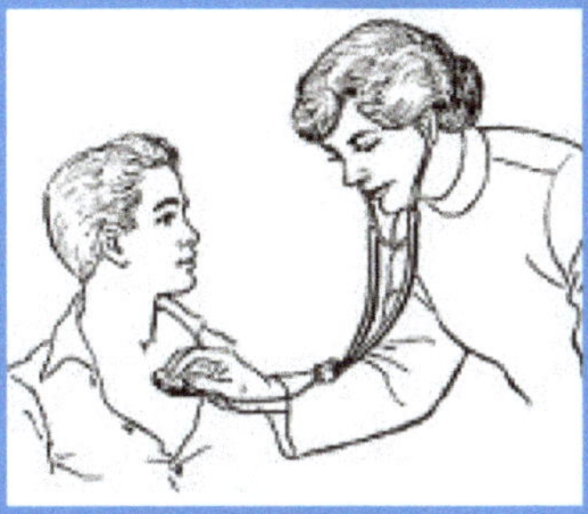

Draw the sentence (Disegna la frase): Un dolce delizioso

The letter e (La lettera e)

ELEFANTE

Practice and Fun (Esercizio e divertimento)

Colour the three pictures that begin with e. (Colora i 3 oggetti che iniziano con e)

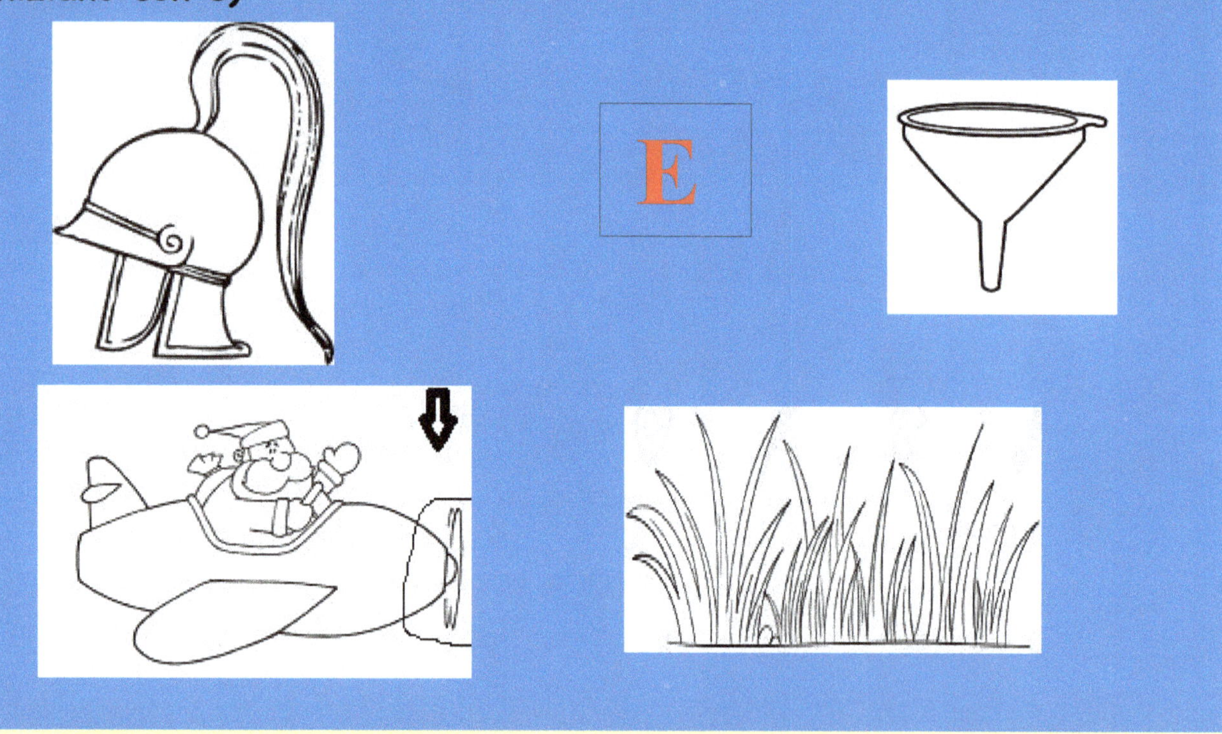

Draw the sentence (Disegna la frase): L'elefante mangia l'erba

The letter f (La lettera f)

FUOCO

Practice and Fun (Esercizio e divertimento)

Colour the five pictures that begin with f. (Colora i 5 oggetti che iniziano con f)

*Draw the sentence (Disegna la frase):*Una farfalla su un fiore

The letter g (La lettera g)

Practice and Fun (Esercizio e divertimento)

Colour the five pictures that begin with g. (Colora i 5 oggetti che iniziano con g)

*Draw the sentence (Disegna la frase):*Una giraffa gialla

The letter h (La lettera h)

HOTEL

Practice and Fun (Esercizio e divertimento)

Colour the two pictures that begin with h. (Colora i 2 oggetti che iniziano con h)

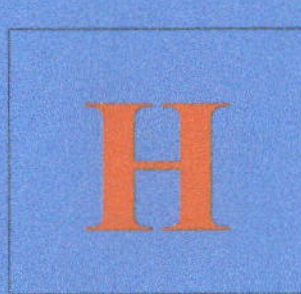

Draw the sentence (Disegna la frase):Un Hotel sull'Himalaya

The letter i (La lettera i)

INSETTI

Practice and Fun (Esercizio e divertimento)

Colour the five pictures that begin with i. (Colora i 5 oggetti che iniziano con i)

*Draw the sentence (Disegna la frase):*Gli insetti sull'igloo

The letter *l* (La lettera *l*)

LIBRO

Practice and Fun (Esercizio e divertimento)

Colour the five pictures that begin with *l* . (Colora i 5 oggetti che iniziano con *l*)

Draw the sentence (Disegna la frase): Il Lupo saluta la luna

The letter m (La lettera m)

MATITA

Practice and Fun (Esercizio e divertimento)

Colour the five pictures that begin with m. (Colora i 5 oggetti che iniziano con m)

Draw the sentence (Disegna la frase): Una matita nelle mani

The letter n (La lettera n)

NUVOLA

Practice and Fun (Esercizio e divertimento)

Colour the five pictures that begin with n. (Colora i 5 oggetti che iniziano con n)

*Draw the sentence (Disegna la frase):*Una nuova nave

Play with rhymes (Gioca con le rime)

PIATTO	RATTO	GATTO

Learning with fun

Colour the 2 pictures that rhyme on each line (Colora le 2 parole che in ogni linea fanno rima)

BASTONE	LIMONE	LAMPADINA

CIOCCOLATO	GELATO	LATTUGA

BILANCIA	ARANCIA	VALIGIA

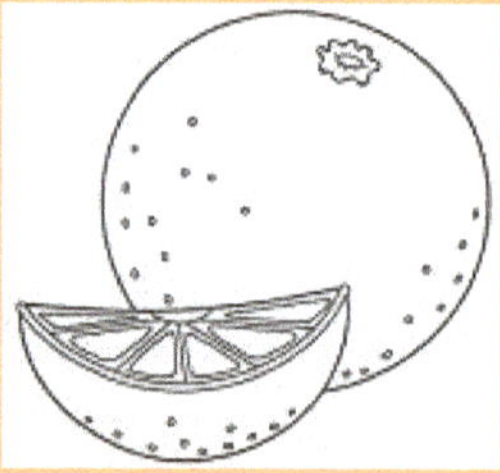

Draw the sentences (Disegna le frasi):

1)Un'arancia sulla bilancia

2)Una conchiglia nella bottiglia

The letter o (La lettera o)

OCCHIALI

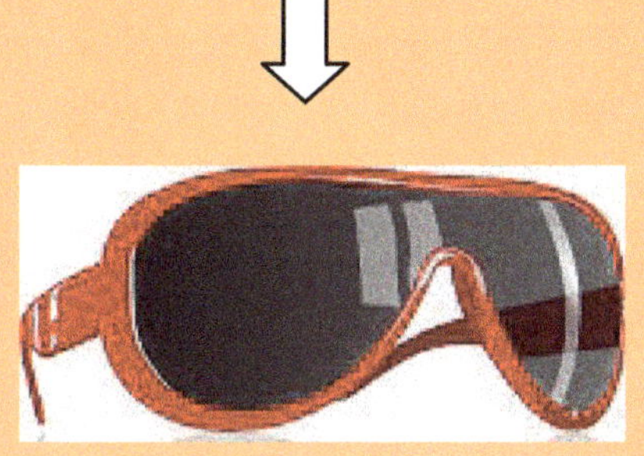

Practice and Fun (Esercizio e divertimento)

Colour the four pictures that begin with o. (Colora i 4 oggetti che iniziano con o)

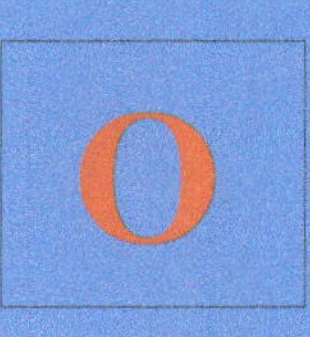

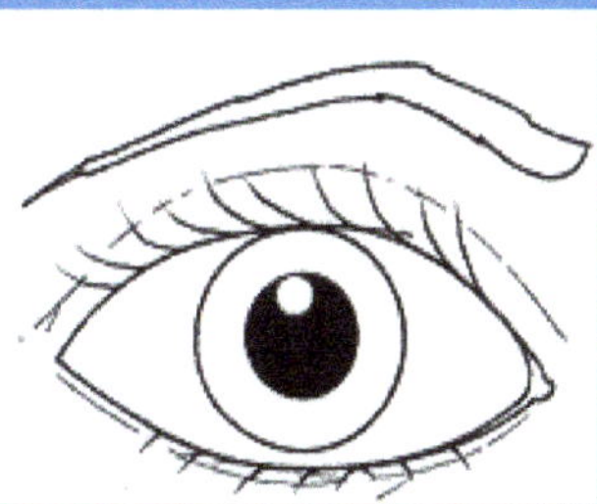

Draw the sentence (Disegna la frase):Un orso e la sua ombra

The letter p (La lettera p)

Practice and Fun (Esercizio e divertimento)

Colour the five pictures that begin with p. (Colora i 5 oggetti che iniziano con p)

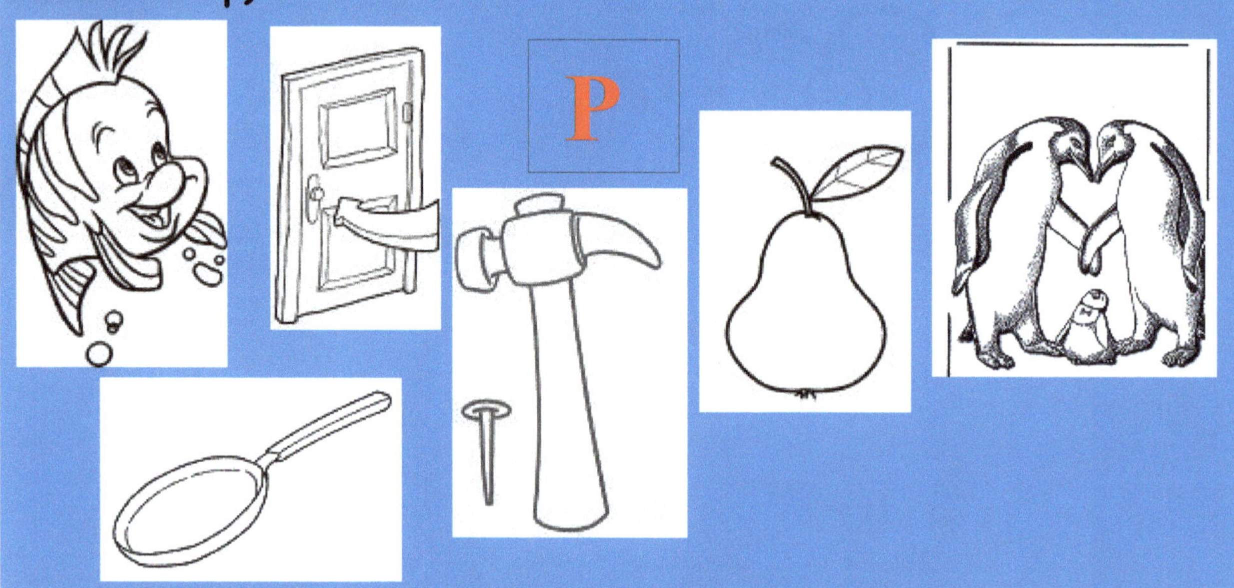

*Draw the sentence (Disegna la frase):*Un pappagallo puzzolente

The letter q (La lettera q)

QUADRO

Practice and Fun (Esercizio e divertimento)

Colour the three pictures that begin with q. (Colora i 3 oggetti che iniziano con q)

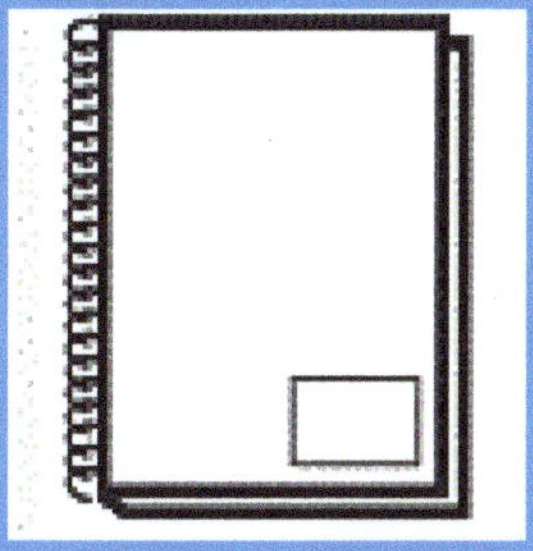

*Draw the sentence (Disegna la frase):*Un quadro con un quadrifoglio

The letter r (La lettera r)

RANA

Practice and Fun (Esercizio e divertimento)

Colour the five pictures that begin with r. (Colora i 5 oggetti che iniziano con r)

R

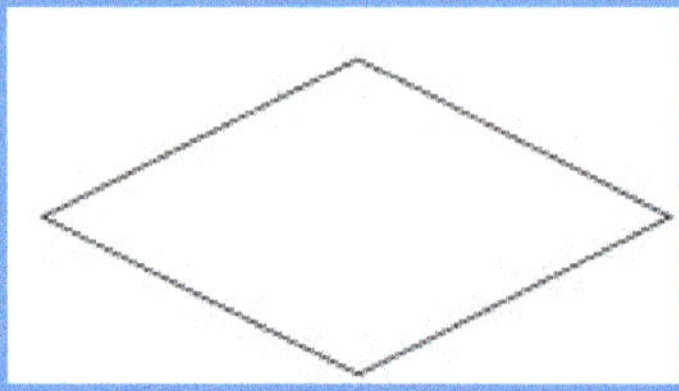

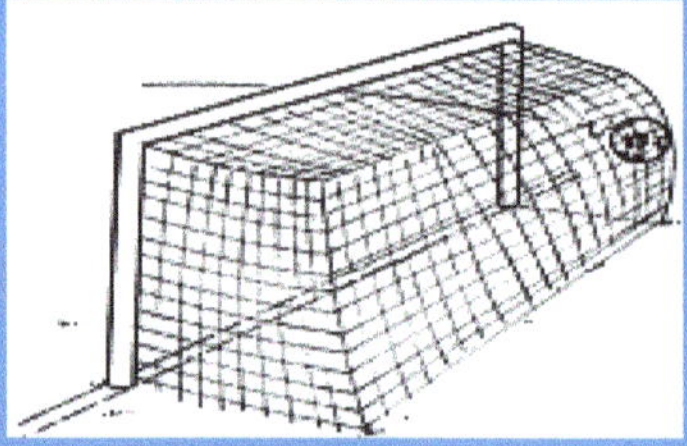

*Draw the sentence (Disegna la frase):*Una renna rosa

The letter s (La lettera s)

Practice and Fun (Esercizio e divertimento)

Colour the five pictures that begin with s. (Colora i 5 oggetti che iniziano con s)

Draw the sentence (Disegna la frase):Un serpente stanco

The letter t (La lettera t)

TARTARUGA

Practice and Fun (Esercizio e divertimento)

Colour the five pictures that begin with t. (Colora i 5 oggetti che iniziano con t)

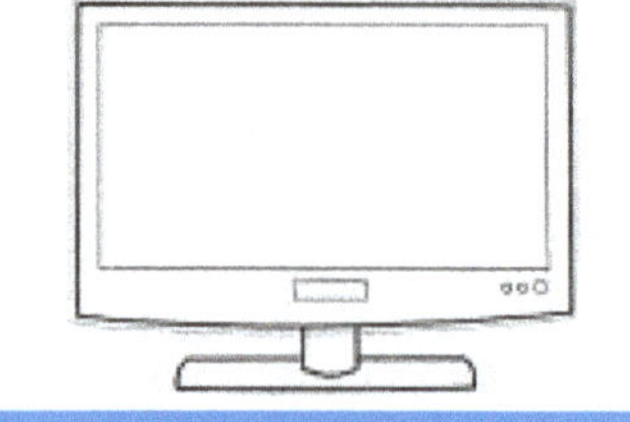

Draw the sentence (Disegna la frase): Tre televisori

The letter u (La lettera u)

UVA

Practice and Fun (Esercizio e divertimento)

Colour the three pictures that begin with u. (Colora i 3 oggetti che iniziano con u)

*Draw the sentence (Disegna la frase):*L'uovo di un uccello

The letter v (La lettera v)

VIOLINO

Practice and Fun (Esercizio e divertimento)

Colour the five pictures that begin with v. (Colora i 5 oggetti che iniziano con v)

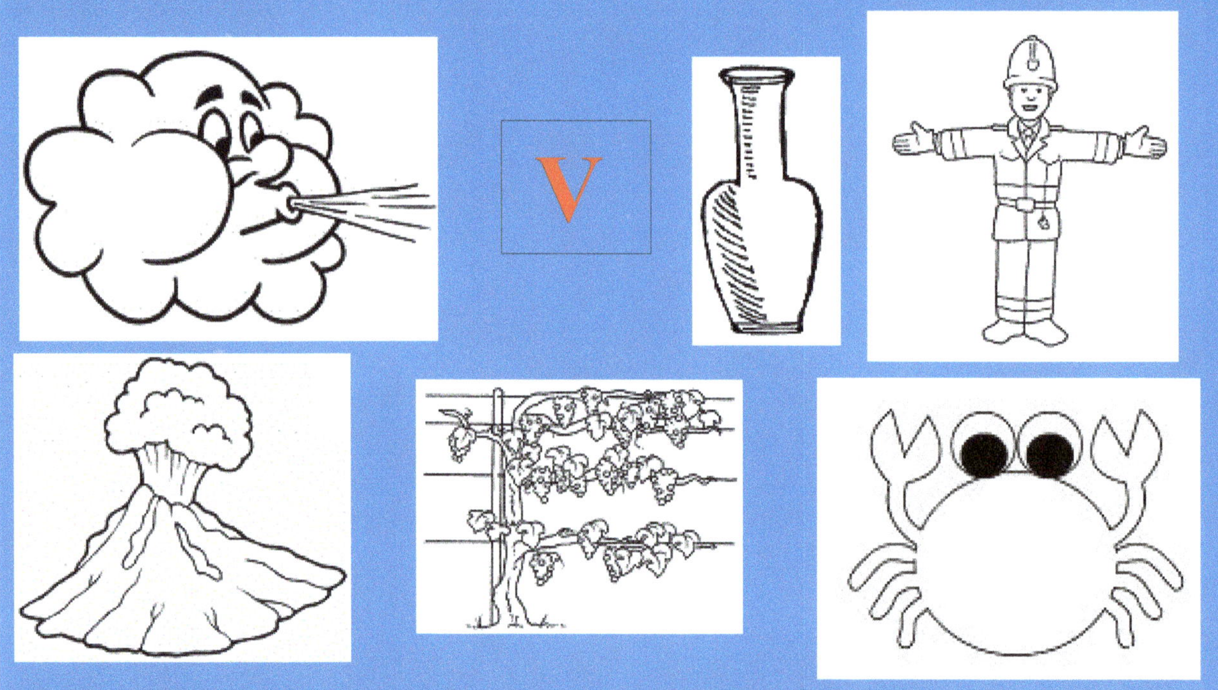

Draw the sentence (Disegna la frase): Una valigia verde

The letter z (La lettera z)

ZEBRA

Practice and Fun (Esercizio e divertimento)

Colour the three pictures that begin with z. (Colora i 3 oggetti che iniziano con z)

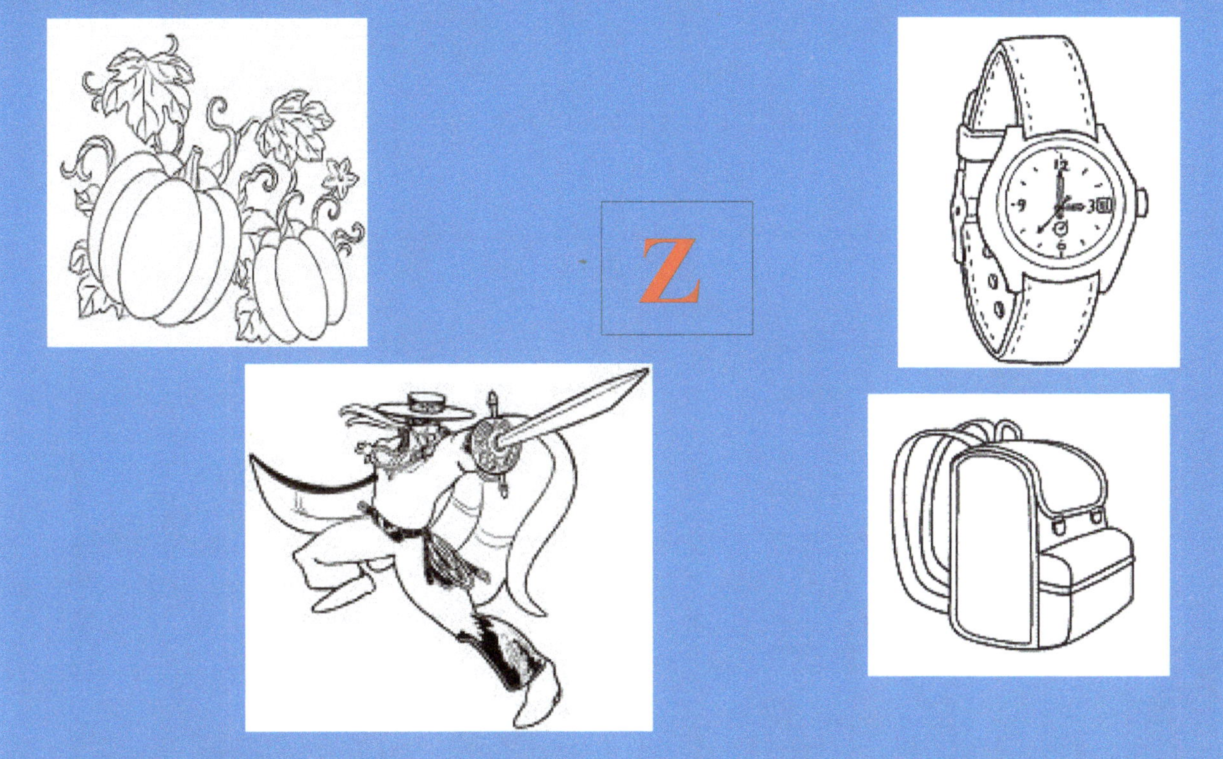

Draw the sentence (Disegna la frase):Una zebra in uno zoo

Practice Tests (Prove di verifica)

Fill with the missing letters (Completa con le lettere mancanti)

1) VUL _ AN_   2) O_O_OGI_   3) _EC_O 4) ZA_NO
5) _OR_O 6) ZU_CA 7) _ATT_GA 8) OM_RE_LO

Summary (Riassunto)

Pronunce the name of each picture below (Pronuncia il nome di ogni oggetto)

GLOSSARY (GLOSSARIO)

A
Aereo:Airplane
Albero: Tree
Ananas: Pineapple
Ancora: Anchor
Ape: Bee
Arancia:Orange
Arco:Bow
B
Bandiera: Flag
Bastone: Walking stick
Becco: Beak
Bilancia:Scale
Borsa: Bag
Bottiglia: Bottle
Bottone:Button
C
Camicia: Shirt
Cane: Dog
Cappello: Hat
Carota: Carrot
Casa: Home
Cavallo: Horse
Coniglio: Rabbit
Cuore: Heart
D
Dado: Die
Delfino: Doplhin
Delizioso: Delicious
Denaro: Money
Dinosauro:Dinosaur
Dolce: Cake
Dottoressa: Doctor
E
Elefante: Elephant
Elica:Propeller
Elmo: Helmet
Erba: Grass

F
Farfalla: Butterfly
Fuoco: Fire
Finestra:Window
Fiore: Flower
Forchetta: Fork
Formica: Ant
Fragola: Strawberry
Fungo: Mushroom
G
Gallina: Hen
Gamba:Leg
Gatto: Cat
Gelato: Ice-Cream
Giubbotto:Jacket
Granchio: Crab
Grillo:Cricket
H
Hockey: Hockey
Hostess: Hostess
Hotel(Albergo): Hotel
I
Igloo:Igloo
Imbuto: Funnel
Inchiostro: Ink
Insetto: Insect
Ippopotamo: Hippopotamus
Isola: Isle
Italia: Italy
L
Lampadina: Light Bulb
Lattuga: Lettuce
Libro: Book
Limone: Lemon
Luna: Moon
Lupo: Wolf
M
Maiale: Pig
Mano: Hand
Mare: Sea
Marinaio: Sailor

Martello: Hammer
Matita: Pencil
Mela: Apple
Mongolfiera: Hot air Baloon
Mucca: Cow

Nave: Ship
Neve: Snow
Nido: Nest
Noce: Walnut
Nove: Nine
Nuova: New
Nuvola: Cloud
O
Occhiali:Glasses
Occhio: Eye
Orecchio: Ear
Ombra: Shadow
Ombrello: Umbrella
Orologio: Clock
Orso: Bear
Otto: Eight
P
Padella: Pan
Palla: Ball
Pane: Bread
Pera: Pear
Pesce: Fish
Piatto: Dish
Pinguino: Penguin
Porta: Door
Puzzolente: Stinking
Q
Quaderno: Notebook
Quadrato: Square
Quadrifoglio: Four-leaved
Quadro: Painting
R
Rana: Frog
Ratto: Rat
Renna: Reindeer

Rete: Net
Rinoceronte: Rhino
Robot: Robot
Rombo: Rhombus
Rosa: Pink
Rospo: Toad
S
Salutare: to greet
Sedia: Chair
Serpente: Snake
Sette: Seven
Sicilia: Sicily
Siringa: Syringe
Sole: Sun
Sottomarino: Submarine
Stanco: tired
T
Tamburo: Drum
Tartaruga: Turtle
Tavolo: Table
Tenda da campeggio: Tent
Telefono:Telephone
Televisore: Tv
Torcia: Flashlight
Toro: Bull
Tre: Three
Treno: Train
U
Uccello: Bird
Unghia: Nail
Uovo: Egg
Uva: Grape
V
Valigia: Suitcase
Vaso: Vase
Vento: Wind
Verde: Green
Vigile:Traffic policeman
Violino: Violin
Vite: Grapevine
Vulcano: volcano

Z

Zaino: Backpack
Zebra: Zebra
Zoo: Zoo
Zorro: Zorro
Zucca: Pumpkin

Titolo | Io non parlo Italiano. I don't speak Italian
Autore | Matteo Albarella

ISBN | 978-88-91197-32-0

Youcanprint Self-Publishing
Via Roma, 73 - 73039 Tricase (LE) - Italy
www.youcanprint.it
info@youcanprint.it
Facebook: facebook.com/youcanprint.it
Twitter: twitter.com/youcanprintit

Finito di stampare nel mese di Luglio 2015
per conto di Youcanprint *Self - Publishing*